D0467774

Plus

Understanding Differences

Some Kids Wear
Leg Braces

Revised Edition

4D

Download the
Capstone 4D app
for additional content.

4D See page 2
for directions.

by Lola M. Schaefer

CAPSTONE PRESS
a capstone imprint

Download the Capstone 4D app!

- Ask an adult to search in the Apple App Store or Google Play for "Capstone 4D".
- Click Install (Android) or Get, then Install (Apple).
- Open the app.
- Scan any of the following spreads with this icon:

When you scan a spread, you'll find fun extra stuff to go with this book!
You can also find these things on the web at www.capstone4D.com
using the password: **braces.09991**

Pebble Plus is published by Capstone Press,
1710 Roe Crest Drive, North Mankato, Minnesota 56003
www.mycapstone.com

**Library of Congress Cataloging-in-Publication Data is
available on the Library of Congress website.**
ISBN 978-1-5435-0999-1 (library binding)
ISBN 978-1-5435-1003-4 (paperback)
ISBN 978-1-5435-1007-2 (ebook pdf)

Editorial Credits
Sarah Bennett, designer; Tracy Cummins, media researcher;
Tori Abraham, production specialist

Photo Credits
Capstone Studio: Karon Dubke, Cover, 5, 9, 11, 13, 15, 17, 21;
Getty Images: KidStock, 7; iStockphoto: duaneellison, 19;
Shutterstock: DoozyDo, Design Element

Note to Parents and Teachers

The Understanding Differences set supports national social
studies standards related to individual development and
identity. This book describes and illustrates children who wear
leg braces. The images support early readers in understanding
the text. The repetition of words and phrases helps early readers
learn new words. This book also introduces early readers to
subject-specific vocabulary words, which are defined in the
Glossary section. Early readers may need assistance to read
some words and to use the Table of Contents, Glossary, Read
More, Internet Sites, Critical Thinking Questions, and Index
sections of the book.

Printed in the United States of America.
010775S18

Table of Contents

How Leg Braces Help

Some kids wear leg braces.

Leg braces support
weak or injured legs.

Leg braces help kids
stand and move.

Some kids who wear

leg braces are born

with weak bones or muscles.

Other kids wear leg braces

because they got hurt.

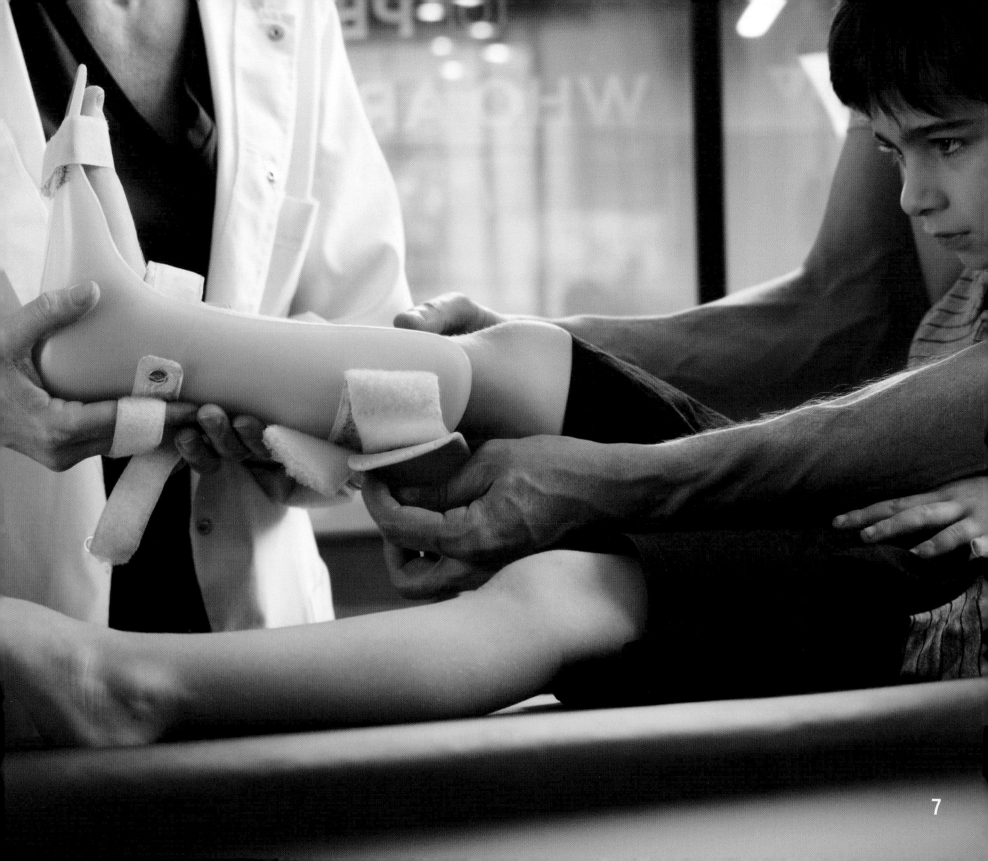

Some kids start wearing
leg braces when they are
very young.

9

Leg braces are different colors
and sizes.
Leg braces cover
the whole leg or
only part of the leg.

Physical therapists teach kids

to use leg braces.

They teach kids how

to exercise and move.

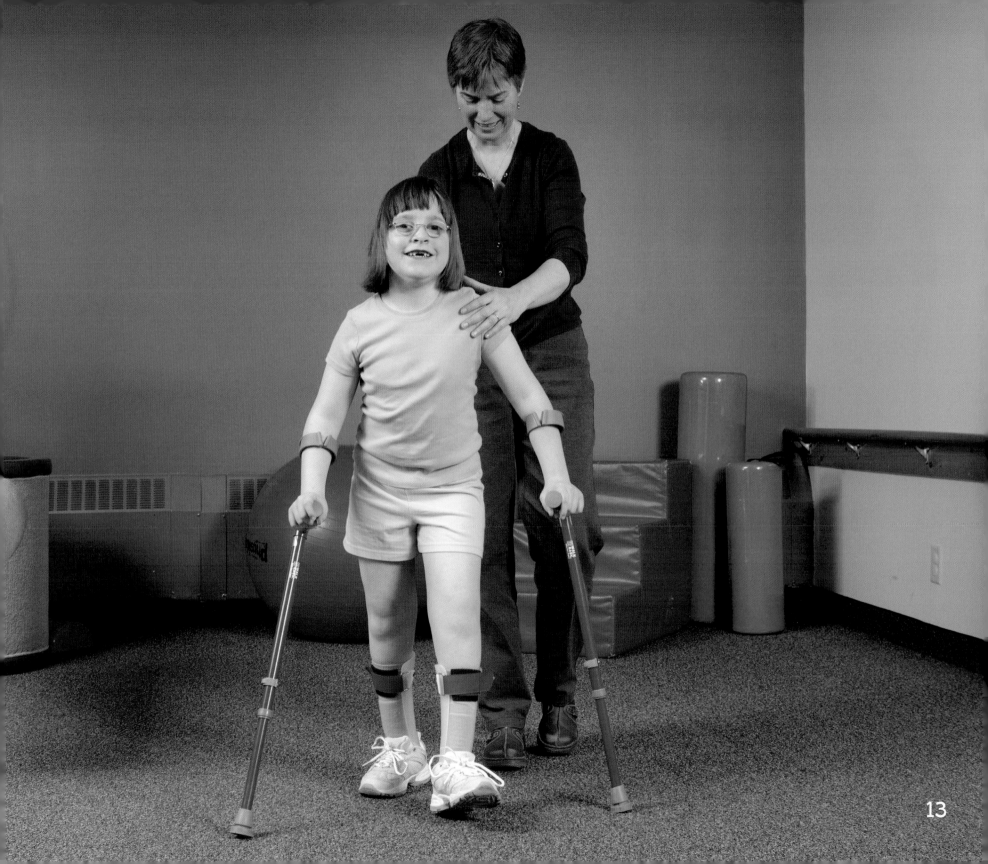

Everyday Life

Some kids who wear

leg braces use walkers

or crutches.

They go for walks.

Kids who wear leg braces help at home.

They dust or do other jobs.

Kids who wear leg braces
study and do homework.

Kids who wear leg braces like
to have fun.
They play with their friends.

Glossary

crutch—a long wooden or metal stick with a padded top; people with leg injuries often use crutches to help them walk

exercise—physical activity that a person does to keep fit and healthy

injured—damaged or hurt; some people wear leg braces because they were injured

physical therapist—a person trained to give treatment to people who are hurt or have physical disabilities; massage and exercise are two kinds of treatment

support—to help hold something in place; leg braces support weak joints and injured legs and feet

walker—a metal frame with four legs and wheels that supports people when they walk; walkers improve balance and stability

Read More

Burcaw, Shane. *Not So Different.* New York: Roaring Brook Press, 2017.

Higgins, Melissa. *We All Have Different Abilities.* Celebrating Differences. North Mankato, Minn.: Capstone Press, 2012.

Pettiford, Rebecca. *Different Abilities.* Celebrating Differences. Minneapolis: Jump!, Inc., 2017.

Internet Sites

Use FactHound to find Internet sites related to this book.

Visit www.facthound.com

Just type **9781543509991** and go.

 Check out projects, games and lots more at
www.capstonekids.com

Critical Thinking Questions

1. Describe reasons why some kids wear leg braces.

2. How does wearing leg braces help some kids?

3. What does a physical therapist do to help kids who wear leg braces?

Index